PRIVATE GARDENS
of SANTA BARBARA

PRIVATE GARDENS
of SANTA BARBARA

THE ART OF OUTDOOR LIVING

MARGIE GRACE

PHOTOGRAPHS BY HOLLY LEPERE

GIBBS SMITH
TO ENRICH AND INSPIRE HUMANKIND

The gardens in this book share a common thread.
No matter the project style, size, or budget, these gardens were created in
collaboration with clients who were committed to extraordinary results.

With deepest gratitude to our clients—
for their trust, their generosity of spirit, and their commitment to excellence.

Contents

Introduction

I am a garden maker.

The job is an important one. Vital, in fact. Gardens connect us to nature. They offer beauty and inspiration. They sustain the birds and the bees. They sustain us. Done well, gardens send the soul soaring.

We are creatures of nature. As such, we need to connect with nature. Deeply. Daily. To recharge our batteries, to feed our spirit, to inspire our dreams, to breathe in the oxygen exhaled by plants.

Few of us, however, live the life of Thoreau on Walden Pond. We live near our jobs and our schools and sometimes our families. Usually in areas that are far removed from wildland. We get the critical nature fix we need from the gardens we build. Our gardens bring nature to our doorstep and connect us with the larger environment. Great gardens pull us irresistibly into the outdoors—to feel the warmth of the sun on our skin, to hear the birds sing, to lie in the shade with a book, to stop and smell the roses.

Most of us live in cities, suburbs, or villages consisting of both built and natural environments that call forth certain behaviors and emotions. A busy urban center with chaotic traffic, for instance, leaves us feeling stressed out. A serene garden fosters a tranquil feeling. A well-organized office supports productivity. A whimsical space encourages playfulness. A place of beauty makes our heart sing.

To make a truly great garden, one that rocks our world, requires listening keenly to the land and to the people who use the space. The landscapes pictured in these pages range from intimate gardens to large

estates and run the gamut from sublime and naturalistic to bold and urban. Styles range from traditional to contemporary, romantic to whimsical, restrained to unapologetically exuberant. What they have in common, however, is what makes them truly great: each is a response to the unique character of the site, the architecture, and the larger environment, adapted to fit the lifestyle, personality, and practical needs of the people who live there.

As you peruse the images in this book, I invite you to take ideas and inspiration for your own garden making.

Margie Grace

Sea Cliff

Avid and accomplished sailors, these homeowners were immediately smitten by this spectacular bluff-top site with its panoramic ocean, island, and mountain views. The existing house was to receive a complete make-over. The landscape, I was informed, was to be "midcentury mid-Pacific." With a couple of photos provided by the owner to guide the vision—one of a calm sea dotted with islands at sunset, another of a Japanese woodblock print that put me in mind of waves—the design process was begun. A design that included movement, a rolling floor plane, a few Asian notes, and some drought-tolerant, tropical-feel plantings—with lots of amenities for enjoying being outdoors—ought to do the trick.

The design solutions are natural and repetitive. Landscape mounds evoke dunes, emphasizing the seaside location and hearkening back to the inspiration photos of waves and islands. Broad concrete pavers are used throughout the garden to create different effects: massed together, they provide seating areas; blended with recycled materials, they form a rich mosaic underfoot; and set as single brushstrokes, they lead the eye to the expansive views. A spectacular bier-garten-style bench is suspended over the cliff on I-beams (left behind when an old deck tumbled into the abyss). Sand-filled trays between the beams provide a "beach" to delight bare toes—and to prevent anyone from accidentally slipping over the edge. Sitting at this table, soaring high above the waves with the wind blowing off the ocean, takes your breath away. The experience creates an illusion of being in a swift-sailing boat. This is a magical place to enjoy vibrant sunsets, passing hang gliders, and migrating whales.

Plantings were selected for erosion control, low water demand, high habitat value, and aesthetics.

A narrow biergarten-style table and bench are suspended over the cliff's edge, providing a bird's-eye view of the beach below.

A fieldstone bench does double duty as a retaining wall and as fireside seating. Steel I-beams, remnants of an old deck, were integrated into the patio paving.

LEFT: Broad concrete pavers lead to the entertaining area and draw the eye to the expansive view.

ABOVE: The hot tub is perched on preexisting infrastructure, allowing it to be located at the cliff's edge without disturbing the highly erodible bluff.

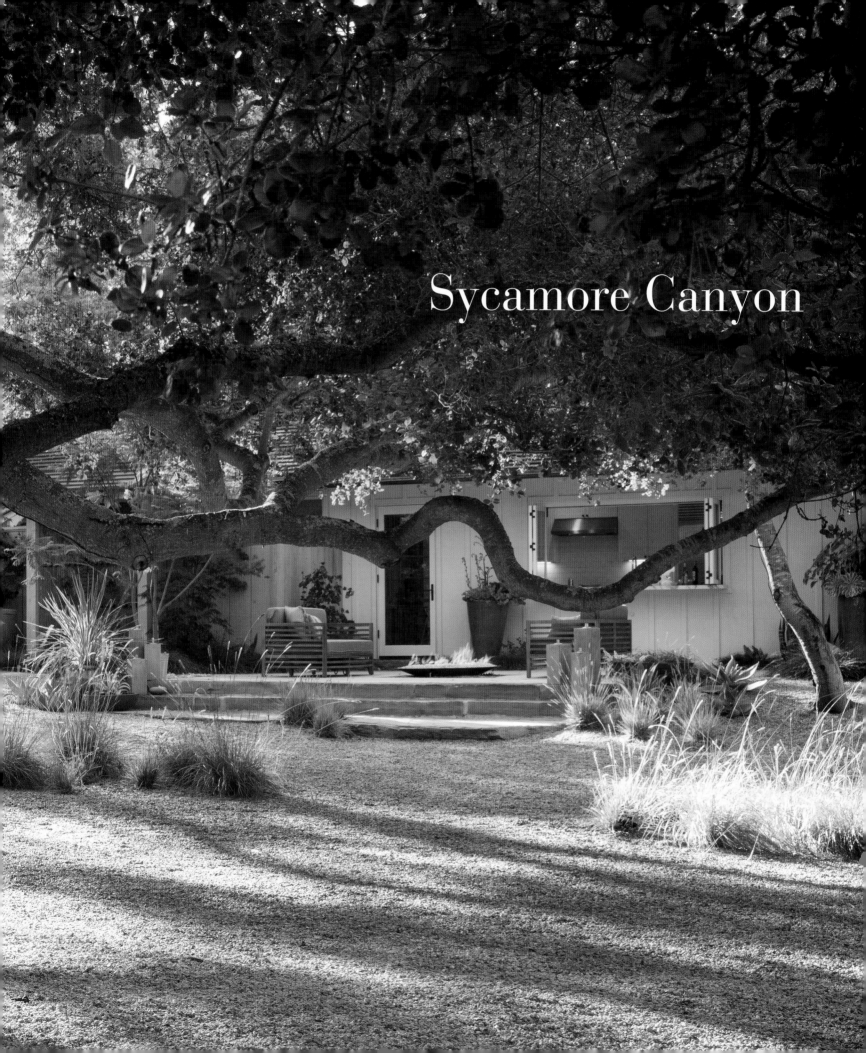

Sycamore Canyon

This, my own garden, takes its inspiration from the world-renowned gardens at Lotusland, my neighbor to the north. Plantings reminiscent of San Ysidro Ranch's cottage gardens and favorite bits of gardens I've built for others are sprinkled in as well. It is a low-water-demand, low-maintenance, fire-smart garden designed to provide comfortable outdoor living day and night, 365 days a year.

Similar to Lotusland, the property is divided into distinct spaces, each with its own themed garden, ranging from whimsical to sublime.

Lotusland South is a terraced garden organized around a central fountain on axis with the Chilean wine palms (*Jubaea chilensis*) that flank Lotusland's driveway across the street. Blousy pink-tone plantings similar to San Ysidro Ranch are spiced up with a smattering of restrained Patina Farm–style plantings.

The Purple Rain Garden features playful purple hoops (reminiscent of our project at the Greystone Mansion show house) draped with strings of mirrors that send light dancing over every surface.

The Bromeliad Garden houses a collection of colorful bromeliads from Lotusland itself. Replete with colorful furniture, suspended glass baubles, and Seuss-like cephalo-pod-inspired hanging planters, this whimsical space sits in the shelter of a mature coast live oak (*Quercus agrifolia*).

The Secret Garden, an enclosed Asian-style jewel, provides the backdrop for the master bath. The garden features antique Chinese gates, a rustic granite fountain, and speci-men Japanese maples.

The Park, with its grand live oaks, expansive open space, and drifts of ornamental grasses, is exquisite in its beauty and simplicity.

Additional landscape features include a fire pit, a pond, multiple fountains, a living pergola, and landscape lighting.

Outdoor spaces for dining and lounging nearly double the home's living space.

22

LEFT: The Asian-style Secret Garden—a tranquil vignette seen only from the master bathroom—lies beyond these antique Chinese gates.

ABOVE: Asiatic lion (or foo dog) door pulls guard the entry gates to the Secret Garden.

THIS PAGE AND RIGHT:
Golden barrel cactus
(*Echinocactus grusonii*), carrion
plant (*Stapelia grandiflora*), and
'Blue Glow' agave (*Agave 'Blue
Glow'*) in the motor court area.
Shallow water bowls—*tinajas*—
dry out before mosquitoes
hatch.

A driftwood log adds visual interest to the composition and richness to the backyard ecosystem. The log shelters lizards and salamanders and birds forage on the insects that feed on the wood.

Cooled by the nearby pond, this dining area is shaded by a living pergola comprised of sycamore trees (*Platanus racemosa*).

ABOVE: Mix-and-match chairs around the farm table add character.

RIGHT: Slender veldt grass (*Pennisetum spathiolatum*) and other sculptural plants glow in the golden late afternoon light.

Indoor-outdoor living at its best. The line between inside and outside virtually disappears when the doors and windows are open.

A pass-through window provides easy access to the kitchen from the fire pit area.

ABOVE: Vintage wicker chairs on the font porch overlook Lotusland South.

RIGHT: Concrete pavers and Sydney Peak flagstone, seen here in the front yard, are used throughout the property to knit the garden spaces together. The ornate garden gate leads to the motor court area.

A reproduction grotesque from Lotusland guards the entry to this front yard garden, dubbed Lotusland South.

The Bromeliad Garden features colorful furniture, suspended glass baubles, and multihued pots brimming with bromeliads purchased at auction from Lotusland.

Strings of mirrors hang from aubergine arbors in the Purple Rain Garden, sending light dancing throughout the garden.

The Lane

BEACH

This beach house is a favorite destination for a family of five active surfers, boogie boarders, and kayakers. The house met their every need for weekend getaways. The yard, however—a rather dreary pit behind a row of looming boulder riprap surrounded by long-neglected plantings—was singularly uninviting and never, *ever*, *EVER* got used. The homeowners wanted to remedy the situation. More room was needed to physically accommodate their growing children, now preteens and teenagers. The family also needed a place to store their sports and beach gear—preferably near the water, easily accessible but out of sight. Additional landscape requests included an outdoor shower to prevent sand from migrating into the house on wet feet, a fire pit, perimeter screening, new plantings, and pots to enliven the existing deck.

Beach sand was imported from off-site to raise the open portion of the yard nearly two feet. The areas adjacent to and below the existing raised deck were left at the original grade, some two feet lower than the rest of the space. Previously orphaned from the neighboring beach, the now higher yard seems a part of it. The area below the deck provides ample hidden, easily accessible, close-to-the-water storage for beach gear. The new outdoor shower with its split-cedar screening panel is tucked away from view on the side of the raised deck. A new stone bench woven into the existing boulder riprap creates the illusion of a much larger space and brings the boulders into scale with the rest of the landscape. A camp-fire-style fire pit provides a quintessential beach vibe and is now the center of evening activities. Simple, understated, low-water-demand, low-maintenance plantings in shades of blue, silver, and green are well adapted to the sand, salt, and wind and echo the colors of the larger landscape.

Raising the elevation and integrating a stone bench into the existing boulder riprap transformed this dreary backyard into an inviting beachside gathering place.

Concrete and teak chairs by Wells Concrete Works.

Potted succulents withstand the punishing salt, wind, and sun on this seaside deck.

Whimsical Retreat

Having just completed construction on their dream home, this young family shifted focus to creating their dream garden. They wanted outdoor spaces to foster curiosity and fun, to nurture their love of nature, and to enjoy the company of family and friends. Located in the Santa Barbara foothills, they required a fire-smart, low-water, low-maintenance garden to, in their words, "attract birds and bees, but not rattlesnakes and skunks."

Terracing and land contouring were used to make convenient spaces with distinct feels and functions, to create form and flow between garden zones and elements, and to produce broad, slightly depressed areas for capturing rainwater to allow it to percolate into the soil.

The plant palette relies heavily on succulent species, which, once established, require no supplemental irrigation. Drip irrigation is used to efficiently water non-succulent species. The dramatic, sculptural succulents in fantastical forms echo the playful architecture of the home. Massive sandstone boulders and cobbles—grubbed from the site during construction—were used for walls, walkways, patios, and benches, giving the impression that the gardens grew naturally out of the surrounding wild terrain.

Garden elements include shady sitting spots; unthirsty, low-mow, native-grass play lawns; casual outdoor cooking and dining areas; recirculating fountains; dramatic pots; a bocce court; and landscape lighting. Fire-smart features include high-water-content succulents, low-fuel-content plantings, irrigated lawn, expansive areas of gravel, and other stone mulches.

Sculptural succulents, massive boulders, and a variety of stone mulches combine to make this fantastical garden.

ABOVE: A recirculating fountain provides soothing music and water for the local fauna.

RIGHT: Coral aloe (*Aloe striata*) and deer grass (*Muhlenbergia rigens*) dot the boulder-strewn slope above the bocce court.

Bocce court with decomposed granite
playing surface.

The bold shapes of succulents and boulders complement the whimsical character of the house.

Orange-flowered torch aloe (*Aloe arborescens*) and kleinia (*Senecio mandraliscae*).

An unthirsty native bent grass lawn (*Agrostis pallens*) and a tipi provide play spaces for kids and adults alike.

ABOVE: Brilliant red pencil tree (*Euphorbia tirucalli 'Sticks on Fire'*) lights up the slope above the house.

RIGHT: Plants with blue-toned foliage are used to cool down the brilliant red tones in this planting scheme.

Pedregosa

Envisioning a sustainable landscape

around their new uber-green prefab home, this musical and artistic family of four imagined spaces for quiet contemplation, rejuvenation, lively discussions, lovely meals, and musical evenings with friends. In addition, they asked for a garden that required no maintenance and little supplemental water, supported the local fauna, and included "a little bit of home" (Iowa).

Soil was brought in to form topography and create distinct spaces. Walls, walks, stairs, seating, and decorative boulders were made from massive quantities of sandstone excavated on site. New stonework resembles the varied styles seen throughout the neighborhood and nearby Spanish-era mission, suggesting a long history of site occupation. A graveled "stage" with nearby stone amphitheater seating, an extra-large fire pit, and a cedar hot tub complete the list of landscape amenities.

Unthirsty, low-maintenance plantings feature native plants for their high habitat value. Three varieties of grasses provide that "little bit of Iowa" and capture light and movement throughout the garden. A handful of fruit trees and herbs planted near the kitchen provide food and screening from neighbors.

Strong connections between indoor and outdoor spaces are a key to this very functional and frequently used garden. The previously flat, scraped, urban lot now features a sustainable, naturalistic landscape that seamlessly marries the home's contemporary architecture and the neighborhood's historical houses, which date back to the late 1800s.

And the "no landscape maintenance" requirement? We negotiated with the homeowners for a maintenance budget of a half day per month by a two-person crew, and the garden continues to thrive to this day.

Ribbon bush (*Homalocladium platycladum*) screens the open-air house from the street. A simple, gently undulating ground plane of pink Australian racer (*Myoporum parvifolium 'Pink'*) anchors the structure to the site.

Grasses are used extensively throughout the garden—a reference to the homeowners' native Iowa.

Cedar hot tub and amphitheater seating around the fire pit.

Massive sandstone boulder steps provide access to the hot tub and the ideal habitat for cliff-dwelling "hens and chicks" (*Echeveria sp.*).

ABOVE: The borrowed view of the neighboring 1870s water tower is incorporated into the landscape composition.

RIGHT: Rustic stone steps echo the ipe wood steps up to the artist studio.

Zen Garden

Our clients had been planning to build an Asian-style garden on their three-acre estate for more than four years. In fact, they had already gathered a top-notch collection of statuary, urns, lanterns, and other garden objects from around the world. Yet the garden had not actually been designed. Spanning a wide range of styles, traditions, cultures, centuries, and scales, these collected items were to be integrated into a harmonious whole, creating a daunting design challenge.

Construction of the garden would be challenging as well. The space where it was to go had already been determined and was enclosed within a stucco wall and surrounded by stone walks. With access limited by the perimeter wall and finished surfaces that could easily be damaged by construction activities, the use of heavy equipment was out of the question. All digging and grading would have to be done by hand. Plants and other materials would be limited in size by the existing wall openings. Weight would be limited by what could be moved by sheer muscle. The limitations on construction materials and methods further constrained the design requirements.

Despite these challenges, the design of the garden was very successful and the construction was completed without damaging existing surfaces. Pathways and landscape mounding define three distinct spaces in the finished garden, arranged to exaggerate perspective and create the illusion of a much larger whole. Garden objects from the owners' collection are separated to de-emphasize their disparate sizes. Delicate and shapely specimen Japanese maples (*Acer palmatum* varieties) act as a counterpoint to the heavy stone and iron pieces in the garden. And a carpet of Scotch moss (*Sagina subulata* 'Aurea') ties the garden spaces together.

Weathered granite, Sydney Peak flagstone, black and green pebbles, and landscape mounds are used to create the structure of the garden.

A custom-built bamboo screen separates the Asian-style garden from the adjacent covered walk.

ABOVE: View of dry creek. The Balinese pebbles suggest flowing water.

OPPOSITE: A recirculating fountain comprised of a basalt cistern, a bamboo spout, and a hidden water basin is set at the head of the dry creek.

ABOVE: The garden is studded with elements collected from around the world, including an ancient tile dragon and stone etchings mounted on the garden wall.

RIGHT: A large basalt Buddha.

Garden of Eden

After wildfire destroyed their landscape, these homeowners sought to create outdoor spaces that better suited both their lifestyle and aesthetic—and they were keenly interested in landscaping that would reduce the risk of future conflagrations.

Following Cal Fire guidelines, a "lean, clean, and green" zone was created around the house. (Lean = low-fuel-content plants and hardscape. Clean = removing combustible materials, such as dead plants, limbs overhanging the roof, and stored items, such as firewood. Green = high-water-content plants that won't easily catch fire, such as succulents, lawns, and low, nonwoody groundcovers.) A second zone, 30–100 feet from the house, was planted to reduce fuel and to limit the spread of fire.

The lean, clean, and green zone around the house was created by expanding the gravel motor court and brick entry stoop, refurbishing a patch of lawn, and adding noncombustible hardscape. Plantings in this zone are limited to succulents and nonwoody plants, and large ceramic pots are used extensively to add color and structure without adding fuel.

New walks and steps now optimize access, circulation, slope stability, and safety. New stone walls and terracing carve out spaces for entertaining, for raised vegetable beds, and for lounging around the new "spool" (larger than a spa, smaller than a pool), which can do double duty by providing water for combating future wildfires using a gas-powered pump that is stored nearby.

The site is alive with a joyful, exuberant plant palette selected for fire resistivity, low fuel content, site suitability, and erosion control. Succulent-filled pots, decorative items, and stone, all used extensively throughout the garden, add to the composition without adding fuel for fire.

Colorful, drought-tolerant plantings and sandstone boulders native to the site are used throughout the garden.

This oval cedar "spool"—used for cool summer dips and warm winter soaks—holds more than 4,000 gallons of water, which can be used for firefighting.

OPPOSITE: A large ceramic pot adds architectural interest to the garden.

ABOVE: Low-fuel-content groundcover surrounds the guest house.

Low-water-demand perennials and non-woody
subshrubs provide color throughout the garden.

This outdoor dining area survived the wildfire intact. Pots and furnishings were added during the garden restoration.

Colorful, non-woody, drought-tolerant plantings were selected for their low fuel content and low water demand.

OPPOSITE: A charming vignette outside the master bedroom. The glazed urn, terra-cotta orbs, and metal furniture punch up the design without adding fuel for fire.

Villa Del Greco

Designed in the 1920s by noted architect George Washington Smith, this home and surrounding garden were once part of the architect's personal residence. The lot was formed when the original estate was divided into smaller parcels and contains portions of the original landscape, as well as the architect's original design studio, long since incorporated into a much larger residence.

Looking for a property that called to her and a project to sink her teeth into, the client purchased the home and dove into researching the property's history, intent on refurbishing both house and grounds true to the original design and time period.

Several key issues resulting from the division of the original estate and the subsequent home expansion would have to be addressed in the new landscape design. Wayfinding would have to be improved, as it was nearly impossible to find the front door from the street. Vehicular circulation was awkward as well, and many of the landscape changes made through the years conflicted with the period architecture.

Garden elements from the 1920s—a fabulous allée of black acacias (*Acacia melanoxylon*), fragments of tiled runnels, and a number of fountains—were restored or, if beyond repair, replicated. Discordant landscape elements were culled from the composition.

An inviting new entry courtyard now provides clear guidance to the front door. The driveway has been reconfigured to make a motor court, which resolves the prior constraints on vehicular circulation and provides extra parking. New and refurbished hardscape elements are historically and architecturally compatible with the home's roots, including custom reproduction tile, elaborately patterned brick flatwork, and wrought iron details. Refreshed plantings in vibrant colors reflect the homeowner's choice of color palette.

Two tiled fountains on axis lead the eye to the ridgeline beyond the garden. The fountain piece in the foreground is original to the property.

View toward the street from the new pedestrian-entry courtyard. The custom gate echoes the pattern of the original vehicle gates on the estate.

OPPOSITE: View of the wall fountain from the koi pond. The orange-flowering plant is a dwala aloe (*Aloe chabaudii* var.).

RIGHT: Korean grass (*Zoysia tenuifolia*), blue-flowered Lily of the Nile (*Agapanthus africanus*) and orange-flowered lion's tail (*Leonotis leonurus*).

ABOVE: Assorted succulents in a shell-shaped container.

OPPOSITE: View of the terracotta statue of Bacchus as a youth, from the terrace looking through the black acacia allée.

The guest house—originally an equipment shed—sits at the edge of the koi pond.

Ocean Bluff

This soon-to-be-retired couple was building a beautiful contemporary home with panoramic ocean, island, and mountain views. Their landscape wish list included an outdoor dining area, fire pit, bocce court, turtle pond, and sandy seating area where they could "sit and run their toes through sand." Landscape challenges included wayfinding from street to front door, providing for food cultivation in the inhospitable salt air, and creating privacy for the front yard pool and their nearly see-through house.

The privacy issue was addressed with a frosted-glass fence and gate with a striking modern aesthetic. The fence protects fruit trees and vegetable beds from salt-laden winds and offers up dramatic silhouettes of highly sculptural plantings as well. Dry-laid concrete planks evoke the feeling of a boardwalk, which draws pedestrians through grassy dunes toward a legacy dragon tree (*Dracaena draco*) then on to the front door. The turtle pond features a predator-proof contemporary design, a sleek modern fountain, aquatic plants, and a sand island where the turtles can sunbathe and lay eggs.

A bog adjacent to the pond houses additional water plants, which help maintain healthy water quality. Plants are rotated between the bog and the pond to provide recovery time from grazing turtles. And when the pond is occasionally emptied for cleaning, the pond water flows into subsurface lines to the nearby citrus trees, which thrive on the nutrient-laden water.

A bocce court, cantilevered deck, sand "beach," and native plantings occupy the narrow strip of land on the ocean side of the house, providing low-impact, highly usable space along the bluff's edge.

Additional landscape elements include the owner's sculptures, a fire pit, space heaters, and LED landscape lighting.

An etched-glass fence screens the front yard swimming pool from the street.

THIS PAGE AND OPPOSITE: A colorful sitting area overlooks the turtle pond.

A bocce court, decorative pebbles, pavers, succulents, and native plantings combine to create a very low-water-demand garden rich in detail.

ABOVE: Unthirsty plants and pebble mulch are used to minimize the amount of water used at the top of the bluff.

RIGHT: A small, sandy beach overlooks the ocean and the bocce court.

Terra Bella

These homeowners were just putting the finishing touches on their custom-built home, but were far behind schedule on landscaping. Two years prior, they had offered to host a fundraiser in the garden for four hundred people. The event was now three months off and could not be cancelled. The gardens had to be complete, mature, and ready to receive the well-heeled attendees.

The owners had a number of different landscape plans in hand, none of which actually spoke to their intention for their landscape. They were resolute about their wish for the property to be comprised of ten named gardens, for which they provided a general description and a few inspiration photos. They had also done a lot of buying for their dreamed-of gardens—eighty crates of garden objects, to be precise—although the catalog of items had been lost and they had no recollection of what specifically the crates contained.

Time sped by, with evenings spent designing the next day's work for a crew of twenty. Fountains, walls, walks, statuary, benches, and urns resplendent with plantings took shape in a flurry of construction. At the end of three very short months, all ten gardens stood complete: the White Garden, inspired by the white garden at Sissinghurst Castle; the Sunken Garden, for cut flowers; the Asian-style Zen Garden (see page 85); the Theater Garden, inspired by the Lotusland garden of the same name; the Queen's Garden, home to a giant outdoor chessboard; the Dining Pergola, with seating for thirty; the Herb Garden; the Vegetable Garden; the Vineyard; and the Parterre Garden, inspired by the pattern on a Versace dinner plate provided by the client.

Located on the ocean bluff, this large traditional home required a formal landscape and plants that tolerate the salt air.

A glazed Anduze pot echoes the color of the ocean in the view beyond, pulling the panorama into the composition.

ABOVE: A large copper sugar kettle—now a fountain—is at the center of the Sunken Garden. Matching urns stand at the entrances to the Sunken Garden.

Overview of garden showing
dining pergola, parterre,
Queen's Garden, and tiled
swimming pool.

OPPOSITE: A custom bronze fountain incorporates the straw hat of the owner's father, seen hanging on the back of the chair. His customary summer afternoon snack—bread, fruit, and cheese, with a little *vino tinto* and water—is laid out on the table.

ABOVE: A small vineyard of pinot noir grapes. Roses at the end of each row provide early warning of fungal disease that might affect the vines.

The larger-than-life chessboard in the Queen's Garden is a frequent site of all-day tournaments with family and friends.

Victoria
Garden Mews

Located in downtown Santa Barbara's historic El Pueblo Viejo neighborhood, this project required balancing sustainable design and high-density use with local zoning, historical preservation, and building requirements.

Three couples came together to create this multifamily housing project. Nearing retirement, they wanted to move from the suburbs into the downtown area, where they would be close to services and would be able to make use of public transportation. Their goals were to build the greenest project possible and form a mutually supportive community where they could age in place.

Innovative site planning reduced paved surfaces for vehicles from 42 percent of the lot to 7 percent, freeing up land for landscaping. Flourishing habitat for native fauna, abundant food production, and custom-designed elements to fulfill each resident's specific landscape needs sustain this specialized urban community. Quiet outdoor spaces relieve urban stresses. A large central gathering space fosters relatedness and community building.

Green features include photovoltaic panels, car lifts, electric vehicle charging stations, and bicycle storage. Sustainable landscape features include a 14,000-gallon-capacity rainwater collection system, a dual-supply irrigation system, innovative high-pressure subsurface irrigation, a smart irrigation controller with an on-site weather station, permeable paving, storm water infiltrators, composters, beehives, and custom night-sky-friendly LED landscape lighting.

The project is LEED Platinum certified and is the first residential project worldwide to receive Sustainable Sites Initiative (SITES) certification in the SITES Pilot Project. As of this writing, it remains the only extant SITES-certified multiresidential project in the world.

The cottage-style borders require little supplemental water due to the summer marine layer.

OPPOSITE: A traditional-style garden was required in front of the refurbished Victorian in order to preserve the streetscape in this historical neighborhood. The border plants and turf variety were selected to reduce the water budget.

ABOVE: Harvested rainwater is recirculated in this fountain which masks ambient noise and draws native birds and insects.

The "UC Verde" buffalograss lawn requires half the water of traditional turf species.

A fig-clad arbor screens the neighbor's house from view and provides figs for the whole community.

LEFT: The shared garden space is frequently used for community dinners.

ABOVE: Every square inch of the property is thoughtfully put to use. Here, a narrow recirculating fountain filled with harvested rainwater cools the space, mutes ambient urban noise, supports native fauna, and provides additional seating.

ABOVE: A gently sloping path guides visitors past the communal vegetable garden to the entry foyer of the rear building.

RIGHT: Wheelchair-friendly stabilized decomposed granite walks allow the residents to age in place. The laser-cut recycled copper wall panel is backlit with LED lighting, casting beautiful patterned light at night.

Paseo Tranquillo

I once called this charming 1940s cottage home. I lovingly refurbished the cottage and remade the yard—twice—in the twenty-six years I lived there with my family. The first iteration of the landscaping included a play lawn in the front yard, surrounded by cottage-style borders and an in-ground veggie patch in a remote corner of the backyard. As time passed and my family grew, our needs and priorities changed. A major garden overhaul was required to support our changing lifestyle.

The play lawn was no longer being used and we needed more outdoor living space. Out with the lawn and in with a flagstone patio and comfortable furniture. No more water-guzzling turf and no more mowing!

I'd had it with my vegetable garden too. Heavy clay soil. Encroaching shade. And, while I loved the voluptuous fecundity of the garden in the height of the summer growing season, out of season it was a hot mess. I decided to plant the vegetables in large pots in the sunny front yard, dispersing the veggie pots throughout the existing borders. Pots in the curb strip and along the driveway created additional space for producing food. It was a huge improvement—clean-shoe, no-bend gardening! And the beautiful, shapely ceramic pots added color and structure and looked great year-round.

Semidwarf fruit trees were integrated into the once strictly cottage-style beds. A mixture of ornamental and edible plants wrapped the new outdoor "living room" in the front yard. The resultant garden was easy to maintain, user-friendly for my two boys and their cohorts, and a constant source of organic flowers, fruit, herbs, and vegetables throughout the last dozen years we lived in our much-loved cottage home.

A galvanized trough is tucked into the existing flower border and filled with vegetables and culinary herbs.

Shallow bowls of fresh water draw pollinators to increase food production.

OPPOSITE: Fruit trees and vegetables in large colorful pots are integrated into the existing flower borders.

A flagstone patio replaces what was once a water-intensive play lawn in this much-used outdoor "living room."

ABOVE: The first iteration of the front garden included floriferous borders and a play lawn. In this image, the lawn has been replaced with flagstone.

OPPOSITE: Organic flowers, peaches, and tomatoes from the garden.

Hollister Ranch

This Southern California couple craved a place for undemanding, restorative weekends. A place to take a break from their fast-paced business and recharge their batteries. They envisioned a comfortable, relaxed little getaway—small but flexible enough to accommodate their grown children and friends too.

They found their nirvana—a hilltop surf retreat with breathtaking panoramic views—in Hollister Ranch, thirty miles north of Santa Barbara. All it lacked to support their intended weekend lifestyle was "a few killer outdoor spaces" and a means of excluding cows from their small yard.

The landscape takes its cue from the setting. Restrained plantings—drifts of native grasses, succulents, and herbaceous perennials—harmonize with the larger landscape, tying the house to the land. Large olive trees provide shade and buffer the nearly constant wind.

A cedar hot tub tucked into the hillside out of the wind is surrounded by a flagstone patio. A small flash heater provides a warm-water shower nearby for de-sanding before plunging into the hot tub for a post-surf warm-up. Meandering flagstone paths and lyrical fieldstone "tole work" in the graveled floor plane tie the long, narrow garden space together.

A propane campfire-style fire pit draws people outdoors most evenings—for après-surf guitar sessions and conversation. Soft lantern light adds to the laid-back surf-camp ambiance and lights the path between fireside and hot tub.

A ranch-style solar-powered vehicle gate bars cows from entering the space. Driftwood details—a custom surfboard storage rack made by the homeowner, stools around the fire pit, and posts for the hanging lanterns—complete this quintessential surfer's paradise.

Overview of the landscape showing fire pit, sunbathing area, and entry porch. A simple palette of native plants echoes the larger landscape beyond the garden wall.

The cedar hot tub is a popular spot to take in the panoramic view.

Fueled by propane, this campfire-style fire pit is well suited to the rustic site.

Gathering around the campfire with friends and family is the perfect post-surf activity in this laid-back "surf camp."

OPPOSITE: Detail of stone work in gravel.

Chalk liveforever (*Dudleya pulverulenta*).

Native grasses, yarrow (*Achillea millefolium*), and chalk liveforever (*Dudleya pulverulenta*).

LEFT: A driftwood rack keeps surfboards neatly stored. Pebbles below the rack hold the boards in place to prevent dings. The rack is also handy for drying wet suits, towels, and bathing suits.

ABOVE: Sunbathing area.

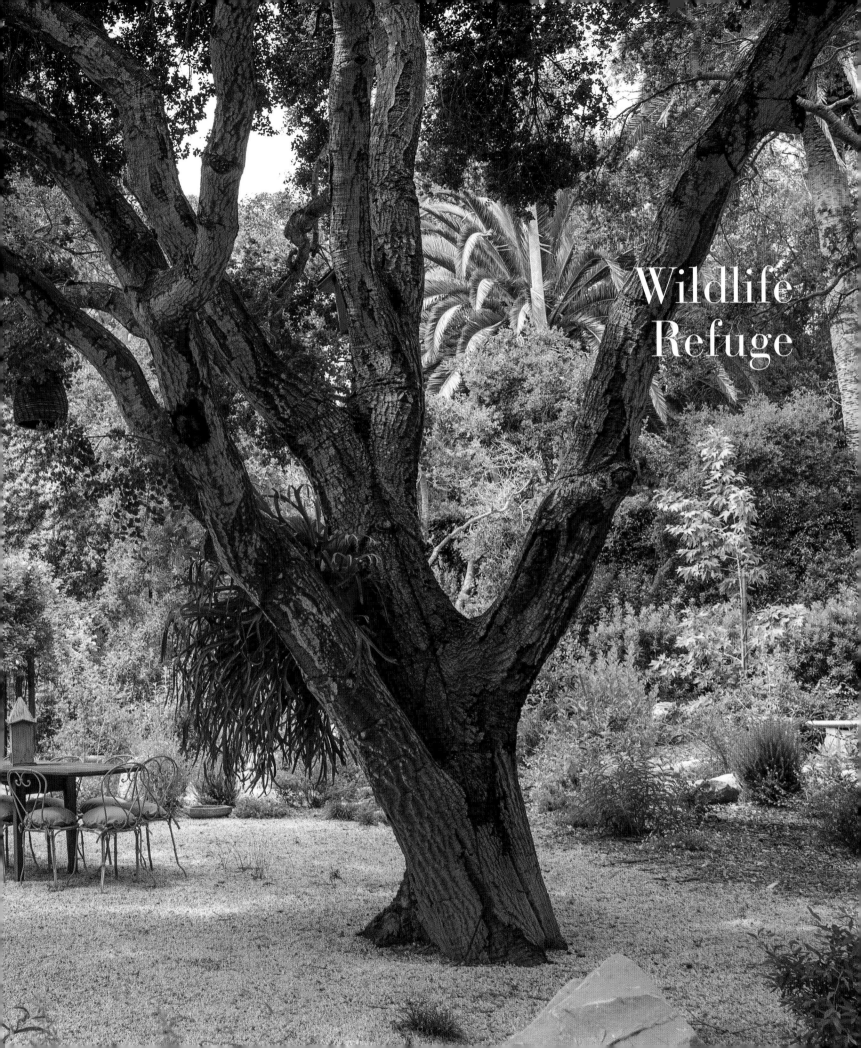

Wildlife
Refuge

The devastating 2018 Montecito Debris Flow left this site covered in three feet of mud and detritus. The images on these pages were taken a mere eight months after the award-winning garden—which we had built in 2004—was restored from the ground up.

Flanked by a large nature preserve on one side and a well-treed estate on the other, the two-acre lot is surrounded by more than eighty-five acres of wooded land. The greenbelt, a vast tract of coastal oak woodland and a stand of eucalyptus used by overwintering monarch butterflies, is home to a range of wildlife.

The homeowners' request, when we built the original garden, was for a landscape that would provide additional wildlife habitat and blend with the larger landscape surrounding the property. After surviving the devastating debris flow, their direction to us was to re-create the habitat and the "garden-y bits too."

A narrow band of "garden-y" plants surrounds the house. Plantings quickly transition from structured to a rich tapestry of wilder, drought-tolerant plants selected for their habitat value. Nesting boxes house bluebirds, bats, and owls. Snags and dead trees provide perches for birds of prey, habitat for grubs, and housing for a colony of honeybees. California quail are prolific, drawn by their favorite native foods, abundant nesting material, and dense, protective shrub cover. The large pre-disaster pond, now restored, attracts a wide variety of native species—mammals, birds, insects, and turtles—and is a favorite nesting site for mallards, whose young are inaccessible to predators in the floating duck houses.

The garden, which has been designated Certified Wildlife Habitat by the National Wildlife Federation, is a constant source of wonder and delight for the homeowners and garden visitors.

Viewing platform at pond.

OPPOSITE: One of the two mallard couples currently using the duck houses on the pond for nesting.

LEFT: California poppies (*Eschscholzia californica*).

ABOVE: A gravel path and broad stone steps lead to the top of Sycamore Hill, a "mountain" built from mud and boulders littering the site after the debris flow.

191

Mallards nest in the floating duck house, where their eggs are safe from predators.

A narrow band of traditional-style plantings embraces the vine-clad structures, quickly giving way to naturalistic plantings that provide habitat for the local fauna.

Motor court and garage.

A pair of rare sphinx statues survived the debris flow. Cleaned and returned to their pre-disaster perch, they stand guard over the entry to the principal residence.

ABOVE: A cast-iron bench in front of the guest house, nestled between potted lavenders.

RIGHT: An antique gate and columns with an espalier apple fence between the main house and guest house.

One of a pair of unique sphinx statues that guard the entry steps of the main house.

This urn and pedestal—salvaged from the debris flow—sits between the guest house and the main residence.

Shadow Hills

Fed up with the gophers and rabbits razing her garden, this accomplished rosarian, avid gardener, and acclaimed author had reached the end of her rope. She would have her super-floriferous patch of paradise or die trying! What she needed was a varmint-free space. Other items on her landscape wish list included easy-access beds (none deeper than could be reached from a path or a patch of lawn), a water element, a permanent shade structure over the existing patio, and a predominantly pink-and-orange color palette.

We terraced the rear yard to stairstep it down the existing slope. We constructed a perimeter wall with a deep footing to exclude critters and installed new garden gates with a scant half inch of bottom clearance to prevent overland access by gophers, rabbits, and voles. Bands of sod and crisscrossing travertine paths arranged along primary, secondary, and tertiary axes keep the owner's shoes mud-free while she tends the narrow, easy-access beds. A central fountain, a broad staircase, urns, and garden gates along the primary axis pull the eye out to the expansive ocean view on the horizon.

Seat walls and a pergola with retractable awnings have been added to the patio, which we expanded and tiled in travertine to match the new hardscape. Benches are placed throughout the garden to encourage stopping to smell the roses. The requested color palette is reflected in the plantings, the custom-colored fountain, the salmon-pink stucco walls, the rose-colored travertine walks, and the terra-cotta pottery.

The formality of the hardscape is in no way mirrored in the plantings. The beds are thickly layered with a barely contained riot of color that perfectly suits the client's personal preferences and lively personality.

The gate at the bottom of the garden provides access to the greenbelt beyond the garden wall.

Colorful plantings thrive within the varmint-excluding walls of the garden.

A colorful fountain sits at the center of the
garden's primary and secondary axes.

A bench outside the garden wall invites passers-by to pause and enjoy the view.

Monarch

A 137-acre preserve comprised of riparian woodland, eucalyptus groves, coastal scrub, grassland, creeks, vernal pools, bluffs, dunes, beaches, and tide pools—home to a large overwintering monarch butterfly population and more than two hundred bird species, including the threatened Western Snowy Plover—provides the backdrop for this unique garden. The homeowners had bought the recently completed home, with its un-landscaped backyard and unadorned central courtyard, as an investment in a yet-to-be-built-out development. They planned to rent out the home's mother-in-law apartment and use the main house as a place to decompress on weekends with their teenage children until they retired, at which time they planned to sell the property.

With such a vast and beautiful natural resource literally at their threshold, I suggested removing the existing perimeter wall to give the illusion that the expansive landscape beyond was an extension of their small backyard. Alas, the perimeter wall was the property of the homeowners association and could not be removed. Committed to visually incorporating the landscape beyond the wall into the home's new backyard landscape, we added soil mounds to hide the perimeter wall, erasing the separation between garden and wildland. Ornamental grasses pull the adjacent grassland into the garden. Plantings support overwintering butterflies. A stone water feature provides soothing notes and water for winged creatures.

Additional landscape amenities include a day bed sheltered beneath a fig-covered pergola, a custom boulder fire pit, a shaded travertine patio, and an interior courtyard replete with travertine flooring, a custom tile fountain, dramatic plantings, comfortable seating, and sumptuous details.

A fire pit carved into a massive sandstone boulder.

A naturalistic gravel walk bordered by unthirsty plantings.

Succulents in a teak bowl grace a custom driftwood-and-glass table.

ABOVE: Potted plants and green-toned furnishings give a garden-like feel to the entry courtyard.

RIGHT: A tiled fountain in the entry courtyard is surrounded by heart-shaped stones collected by the homeowner.

OPPOSITE: A montage of driftwood, tillandsia, found objects, and nearly black Beauverd's Widow's-thrill vine (*Kalanchoe beauverdii*).

A living sculpture comprised of assorted succulents.

The arbor over this daybed will soon be covered in five different varieties of fig, grafted together to form a steel-reinforced arborsculpture.

Hidden Valley

I was surprised to receive an urgent phone call from a woman who declared she was having a "landscape emergency." Never having encountered a genuine landscape emergency before and with my curiosity piqued, I inquired as to the nature of the emergency. "My husband just put a parking lot in my front yard," the caller replied.

Considering that to be a landscape emergency of the highest order, I dashed over to the site to discover that recent construction had left this foothill estate with a vast expanse of new paving, disjunct patches of hardscape, a quantity of haggard plantings, not a lick of flat garden space, and absolutely no clue as to where the front door might be located. Rejecting the idea of removing the majority of the new paving (declaring she "wasn't ready to get divorced just yet"), the homeowner encouraged the development of a plan B to remedy the situation.

A new garden wall matching others on-site creates a motor court and defines a new front garden space. A dramatic, attention-grabbing gate sets visitors on a path past a colorful fountain, through new plantings, and on to a new porch sheltering the front door. A stone bench does double duty as a retaining wall, creating a level floor plane. A drift of elephantine yucca and a large acacia sport a massive staghorn fern, hanging plants, and a chandelier. Olive trees planted along both sides of the new vine-draped garden wall soften its geometry and carve out a cozy reading nook.

A massive outcrop of sandstone and a ceramic urn border the flagstone walk between the main residence and the guest house.

A retaining wall topped with a stone bench was backfilled with soil to provide a level garden space five feet higher than the original grade.

A vintage chair and ottoman provide a
comfortable place to read.

A "garden bed" in the orchard.

Purple aeonium (*Aeonium 'Cyclops'*), red pencil tree (*Euphorbia tirucalli 'Sticks on Fire'*), and blue-toned Kleinia (*Senecio mandraliscae*).

OPPOSITE: Copper aeonium (*Aeonium 'Sunburst'*) and assorted Echeveria and Kleinia (*Senecio mandraliscae*) spill over the brim of a large ceramic pot.

A living table and chair in the orchard area.

OPPOSITE: Table set for breakfast on the guest house patio.

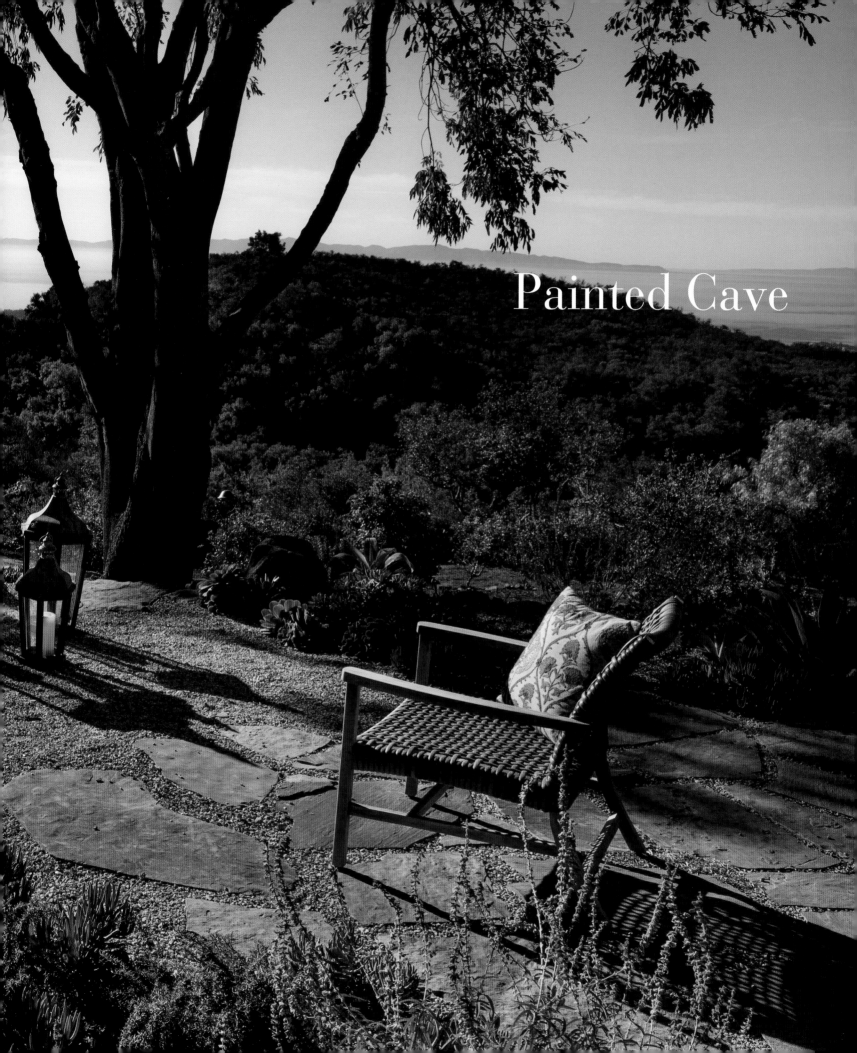

Painted Cave

In search of an escape from frigid East Coast winters, this couple was smitten by the epic ocean, island, and ridgeline views from this secluded hideaway in the mountains above Santa Barbara. The house would require a complete makeover to better suit their lifestyle and aesthetics. Having remodeled homes in the past, they were familiar with the process, but how to go about landscaping in the strange and unfamiliar setting of weathered sandstone outcrops, lean soils, and fire-prone chaparral with limited access to water was a different matter.

The garden surrounding the house is simple and modest in size. Gravel mulch and flagstone, combined with fire-resistive succulents and drifts of low-profile non-woody plantings, provide defensible space around the house for fighting wildfire. Low-fuel-content, low-water-demand, herbaceous plants, with a focus on winter bloom time, blanket the short slope below the house. Beyond this point, landscaping activity is limited to thinning brush and clearing dead fuel to reduce the risk from wildfire.

Flagstone and gravel in the tones of the native sandstone blend seamlessly into the natural setting. The plant list is limited to noninvasive species, eliminating the possibility of damage to the native flora. Occasional pops of color and bold, sculptural plants assert themselves where they won't compete with the views.

Additional site amenities include a propane-fueled cedar hot tub and fire pit, custom stone bench, recirculating fountain to support indigenous wildlife and provide soothing water notes, decorative pots, and several seating areas sited to take advantage of the mind-blowing panoramic views.

A cedar hot tub, stone bench, and sunbathing terrace built into the slope below the residence.

A panoramic view of the Channel Islands off the coast of Santa Barbara provides the backdrop for this garden urn.

Close-up of the stone bench adjacent to the hot tub.

Sunset-viewing terrace adjacent to the south veranda.

LEFT: Mexican sage (*Salvia leucantha*), assorted succulents, and Mexican beach pebbles.

ABOVE: A stone trough fountain.

ABOVE: Entry walk and plantings.

OPPOSITE: Ceramic pots near the entry porch echo the color of the window trim and the dusty blue of the groundcover (*Senecio mandraliscae*).

Awards & Accolades

INTERNATIONAL AWARDS

HIDDEN VALLEY: Association of Professional Landscape Designers (APLD) Merit Award

HOLLISTER RANCH: APLD Merit Award

THE LANE: APLD Silver Award

MONARCH: APLD Merit Award

OCEAN BLUFF: APLD Merit Award

PASEO TRANQUILLO: APLD Special Award

PEDREGOSA: APLD Landscape Designer of the Year

RATTLESNAKE CANYON: APLD Gold Award

SEA CLIFF: APLD Gold Award

SYCAMORE CANYON: APLD Landscape Designer of the Year

VICTORIA GARDEN MEWS: APLD Merit Award

VICTORIA GARDEN MEWS: Sustainable Sites Initiative Pilot Project

VILLA DEL GRECO: APLD Silver Award

WHIMSICAL RETREAT: APLD Gold Award

ZEN GARDEN: APLD Merit Award

NATIONAL AWARDS

BEST OF HOUZZ: 2013–2018

PEDREGOSA: Sunset Dream Garden

VICTORIA GARDEN MEWS: US Green Building Alliance

REGIONAL AWARDS

SANTA BARBARA CONTRACTORS ASSOCIATION CONSTRUCTION AWARDS

GARDEN OF EDEN: Best Landscape & Hardscape

HIDDEN VALLEY: Best Landscape & Hardscape

OCEAN BLUFF: Best Landscape & Hardscape

PASEO TRANQUILLO: Best Landscape & Hardscape

TERRA BELLA: Best Landscape & Hardscape

VICTORIA GARDEN MEWS: Best Landscape & Hardscape

VILLA DEL GRECO: Best Landscape & Hardscape

ZEN GARDEN: Best Landscape & Hardscape

SANTA BARBARA BEAUTIFUL / MONTECITO BEAUTIFUL ANNUAL AWARDS

GARDEN OF EDEN: Large Single Family Residence, Santa Barbara

VICTORIA GARDEN MEWS: Single Family Estate, Santa Barbara

WILDLIFE REFUGE: Montecito Beautiful

INTERNATIONAL LANDSCAPE
DESIGNER OF THE YEAR 2018

The international Association of Professional Landscape Designers (APLD) named Margie Grace 2018 Landscape Designer of the Year—the highest honor in her field.

Margie previously was named Landscape Designer of the Year in 2009 by APLD for the Pedregosa project.

"It is a special honor and privilege to win Landscape Designer of the Year for the Sycamore Canyon garden because it's more than just a project to me—it is also my home. With only myself to please, it was the opportunity to explore and experiment. Why not swing for the fences? I wanted to perfect what I call The Art of Outdoor Living™—the ultimate Santa Barbara lifestyle. I wanted to blur the line between inside and outside and double our living space with lots of outdoor "rooms"—places to enjoy any time of day, any time of year."

—MARGIE GRACE

Acknowledgments

DEEPEST GRATITUDE TO:

The team at Grace Design Associates, for your hard work, your extraordinary artisanship, and your comradery. There could be no better fellow travelers.

John Oberholtzer, for your years of dedication and your innate ability to build and do anything. There could be no better brother.

Karen Strickholm, for your guiding wisdom and your unwavering belief in our enterprise. There could be no better Yoda.

Holly Lepere, for your decades of partnership and your skill at capturing the essence of each garden. There could be no better ally.

Dawn Close, for your support, your vision, and your love. There could be no better partner.

First Edition
24 23 22 21 20   5 4 3 2 1
Text © 2020 Margie Grace
Photographs © 2020 Holly Lepere
except pages 34–35 © 2020 Jim Bartch

Landscape design and construction by Margie Grace, Grace Design Associates, Inc.

Published by
Gibbs Smith
P.O. Box 667
Layton, Utah 84041

1.800.835.4993 orders
www.gibbs-smith.com

Designed by Rita Sowins / Sowins Design
Printed and bound in China

Gibbs Smith books are printed on either recycled, 100% post-consumer waste, FSC-certified papers or on paper produced from sustainable PEFC-certified forest/controlled wood source. Learn more at www.pefc.org.

Library of Congress Cataloging-in-Publication Data
Names: Grace, Margie, author.
Title: Private gardens of Santa Barbara: the art of outdoor living / Margie Grace.
Description: First edition. | Layton : Gibbs Smith, [2020] | Summary: "An invitation into eighteen distinctive private gardens: large estates, modest homes, and surf retreats run the gamut from sublime and naturalistic to bold and urban."—Provided by the publisher.
Identifiers: LCCN 2019022672 | ISBN 9781423654148 (hardcover) | ISBN 9781423654155 (epub)
Subjects: LCSH: Gardens—California—Santa Barbara. | Landscape design—California—Santa Barbara.
Classification: LCC SB451.34.C3 G73 2019 | DDC 635.09794/91—dc23
LC record available at https://lccn.loc.gov/2019022672